# THE HAYFIELD UNION WORKHOUSE
## A History

## by
# JOAN POWELL

GW00771814

ISBN 1 899104 04 8                    26 February 1999

# Introduction

The word "workhouse" still strikes horror in many people's minds even today, sixty seven years after workhouses ceased to exist and the buildings became hospitals, or were put to some other use.

The Industrial Revolution and the resulting migration to the towns made the care of the poor, as introduced in the Acts of Elizabeth I insufficient to cope with industrial unemployment and poverty. In The Case of Labourers in Husbandry by D.Davies an example of weekly expenditure in 1794 for a man, wife and two children was given. For food, candles and laundry 6/2 was required plus 2/8 for rent clothes and medical expenses, a total of 8/10 .The labourer's wage was 7/6, his wife earned 6d and his children nothing,total income was 8/-, leaving a deficit of 10d and probably resulted in a claim for help from the Parish. Poor Law expenditure for England and Wales was £2 million in 1794, but it rose to £8 million by 1818 and was £7 million in 1831 (1). Parishes could no longer raise the sums necessary to cover such an increase and a new way of coping with the poor had to be found. To many the idea of paying money to the able-bodied was an anathema, therefore the workhouse with a strict regime and diet and compulsory work was seen as a deterrent which would discourage the poor from asking for financial help.The aged, sick and very young would accept the workhouse rather than starve, but those who were not prepared to accept the idea would fend for

themselves. Therefore the worker,by selfhelp, would become a more
moral member of society. In practice outdoor relief did not
disappear and workhouses became the home mainly of the old, sick
and very young, with short term stays of the able-bodied
unemployed(2).

> "The workhouse should be a place of hardship, of coarse
> fare, of degradation and humility, it should be
> administered with strict severity:it should be as
> repulsive as is consistant with humanity".

> Rev. H.H.Milman, Vicar of Kendal to Edwin Chadwick(3)

While the new law was meant to ease problems for the
administrators of the old poor law - parish overseers,
magistrates and members of vestries - many of these were against
the reform (4). They argued that workhouses were inappropriate in
towns, as when there was full employment they were not needed,
and when there was unemployment,no workhouse would be big enough
to hold all the claimants of relief(5).
Agitators for industrial reform such as Richard Oastler, Parson
Bull and John Fielden, were also against the Act and described
existing workhouses in Southern England in horrific
terms(6).Hayfield Union in the High Peak of Derbyshire was a
rural union, and in November 1837 a notice called a meeting to
oppose the building of a workhouse (7). This was signed by Lowe
Chadwick, an overseer appointed in 1835 for Beard, Ollersett,

Whitle and Thornsett, at a salary of £40 per annum.

In February 1838, Assistant Commissioner Thomas Stevens wrote to the Commissioners refuting the allegations of Lowe Chadwick and stating that the plan to build a workhouse had already been passed. (8).

Later in the year,Mr.Stevens wrote again saying that" Mr Chadwick was much improved", presumably he had accepted the new workhouse.

The Poor Law Commission set up to administer the new act consisted of three commissioners, Thomas Franklin Lewis, George Nicholls and John Shaw Lefevre, and a secretary Edwin Chadwick. Assistant commissioners were appointed, who were to tour the country and set up the unions and later oversee the running of the workhouses. From the start the Commission met with criticism and after the first five years was renewed on a yearly basis until 1843 when it was once more licensed for five years.(9). The Andover Workhouse Scandal of 1845, when it was revealed that the inmates were starved and treated as less than human,resulted in the Commission being replaced in 1847 by the Poor Law Board, whose president was a Member of Parliament.(10)  It was still believed that central authority for administering the poor law was essential.  In 1871 the new Local Government Board took over responsibility for the Union Workhouses, and in turn was superseded by the Ministry of Health, as now the workhouse had a more hospital orientated role. Old Age Pensions and Workmen's Insurance had to some extent removed the necessity of living in a workhouse because of poverty. The 1929 Local Government Act transferred responsibilty of raising a rate to care for the poor to the County and Borough Councils and the Union workhouse ceased to exist as such after 96 years.

In spite of opposition, the union workhouse eventually became a reality in town and country and the purpose of this paper is to try to answer some of the questions frequently asked such as, what was workhouse life really like, who were the masters and who were the guardians?.

# The forming of the Union and the building of the workhouse

The 1834 Act stated that several parishes should amalgamate to form a Union under a Board of Guardians which would then levy a Poor Rate and administer the money raised.The Assistant Poor Law Commissioners travelled around the country organising groups of parishes into unions and were very involved in the building and every day running of the workhouses.(11)  The Hayfield Union was to include the parishes of Hayfield, Beard, Ollersett, Whitle, Thornsett, Mellor and Disley. The workhouse was to be built at Low Leighton as this was central for the whole union.At first there was little change and the individual parishes continued to operate, though seeking clarification of the new law. The Hayfield Vestry Minute Book 1834-35 records Ebenezer Adamson as Vestry Clerk in the first entry 9th April 1834. A letter signed by him was received by the Commissioners dated 30th October 1834 asking for guidance regarding the treatment of bastards under the new Act and enquiring if it was retrospective. A letter  from the Churchwardens and Overseers of Ollersett, Whitle,Beard and Thornsett, was received by the P.L.C. regarding the appointment of Lowe Chadwick as Overseer. In 1835 James Bowden, Vestry Clerk for Mellor, wrote querying land rating, bastards, paternity payments and salary rises.(12)It was not until 7th December 1837 that the first meeting of the Hayfield Union Board of Guardians took place

Ebenezer Adamson was the Vestry Clerk for Hayfield and Schoolmaster at the Town Day School. In September 1836 it was proposed that he should be the new Registrar of Births and Deaths for Great Hamlet,Phoside, Kinder, Thornsett, Chinley, Bugsworth and Brownside. Lowe Chadwick was put forward by Beard.(13) A letter from P.L.C. in June 1837 stated the Commissioners "would shortly give direction.....regarding the formation of a temporary Registration District which would consist of Great Hamlet, Phoside, Kinder, Whitle, Thornsett, Ollersett, Beard, Mellor and Disley". These were the townships and villages which were to form the Hayfield Poor Law Union. The first meeting of the new Board was held on December 7th 1837 and from this date the Vestries dealt with purely ecclesiastical charity and administrative work. The care of the poor and needy was dealt with by the Guardians. The Guardians met weekly at Low Leighton. Three magistrates, John White of Park Hall, Richard Simpson of Disley and Moses Hadfield, were present at the first meeting at which Thomas Stevens, Assistant Commissioner, took the Chair, together with four Guardians each from Hayfield, Mellor, Disley and one each from Beard, Ollersett, Whitle and Thornsett. Moses Hadfield was appointed Chairman, Thomas Price of Disley was Vice Chairman and Ebenezer Adamson was appointed Clerk to the Guardians at a salary of £50 per annum, subject to the approval of the Commissioners.(14) The Stockport branch of the Manchester & Liverpool District Bank was to act as Treasurer. A Workhouse Committee was set up to look into the building of a workhouse and a Medical Officer and Relieving Officer were to be appointed at

salaries of £70 and £40 per annum respectively. The post of
Relieving Officer went to George Lomas who had previously been an
Assistant Overseer of the Poor.(15)  Ebenezer Adamson's
appointment was confirmed after a letter from Thomas Stevenson
had recommended him as "the best man for the job and completely
trustworthy". (16)

In December 1837 enquiries were made about land at Marsh Lane
Bar, but the owner would not sell. Next,land near Beard Church
was considered and also land belonging to Whitfield
School(Glossop) adjacent to the road from Low Leighton to New
Mills. This latter piece was finally acquired when the
Commissioners agreed to the purchase in November 1838.The site
was central for all villages and townships in the Union.The money
had to be borrowed from private sources as the Treasury fund was
exhausted.(17 )An advertisement was placed in  Manchester,
Stockport, Derby, Sheffield and Chesterfield, in two papers (the
names of which were not given)requesting that plans be submitted
for the workhouse. There is no record of how many plans were
submitted but a plan for a workhouse to house 100-120 inmates,
submitted by Mr. Worth, was recommended by the Guardians to the
Commissioners. While Mr. Worth's name often appears in the
Minutes, no christian name is given or name of a company.The plan
was accepted.A Building Committee was appointed and attended a
site metting with Mr. Worth in July 1838. Sections and
specifications, using a southerly aspect, were requested as soon
as possible. No plan has survived from this time, but the

building has, and, as can be seen when compared to plans of other workhouses of the time, it was a simple design much used.(see illustration).

In September 1838, Thomas Stevens wrote to the Commissioners, "I have been today to Hayfield and enquired their proceedings, I found the Union working remarkably well...". In October 1838 he wrote again asking for a prompt reply regarding the purchase of the site and the building of the workhouse. In early November the reply came with permission to purchase the land. In less than a year in Office, the Guardians had the land and plans to build a workhouse.

The first set of plans contained probationary and vagrant wards and the costs were listed with a total price of £2.300. It had been resolved that no more than £2,000 should be spent , so new plans, minus the probationary ward  at a total price of £2,228 were submitted. Stevens suggested to the Commissioners that  a chapel was not really necessary,and the Commissioners agreed that there was no need for a chapel if there were no  probationary or vagrant wards.They also suggested that the land might be rented instead of bought. After negotiation a lease of 999 years and a rent of £9/9/1 per annum was agreed upon with a right to purchase after 25 years. The workhouse was to be built to a plan drawn up by Dennis Rangeley (Hayfield Guardian and a Builder and Joiner) at a cost of £1,700. Mr. Worth produced revised plans for submission to the Commissioners.

When all was ready to start, the Charity Commissioners wrote
stating that rented land could only be leased for 11 years, so a
999 year lease was not possible. They suggested that the Poor
Rate raised for three years up to Easter 1839 was sufficient to
buy the land at a cost of £236/7/1. The Poor Law Commissioners
agreed that the land could be bought and the price added to the
building costs, the total not to exceed £2,000. The draft
conveyance for the land was signed in December, 1840 and the
Guardians applied to the Economic Life Assurance Society,
Blackfriars, for the money. The previous tenderers for the
building were informed of the modified plans and Mr. Rangeley's
tender was accepted provided he waived any remuneration for plans
and specifications. He signed with his seal and the Chairman of
the Guardians did the same. Economic Life Assurance gave a loan
of £2,000 on the collateral of the Poor Rates. The mortgage was
signed in April and the money received in May. Mr. Higginbottom
was asked to proceed with the conveyance , which was finally
signed in September 1843! Tenders for stoves, brewpans,steamers
iron bedsteads and kitchen ranges were sought as well as
estimates for joinery and furnishing the workhouse.

In the early months of 1841 a single story entrance and porter's
lodge were to be included, beds were ordered and fires were kept
burning in the building to dry it out. The Minutes recorded that
a "pot shelf" was to be placed in the kitchen, and the passage
between the two outer doors......was to be flagged".The building
was insured with the Sun Fire Office for £1,000, for 12 months in

April, and in May, the first Master and Matron were appointed. No definite date of opening is recorded but it must be assumed that the workhouse was open for business shortly after the master was appointed, although the building work on the boundary wall and a pig sty continued after that time. By 1842 a ventilation system had to be installed in the wash house. It was also decided that a Dead House was needed. It was considered that the infirmary should be raised a storey in order better to accommodate the sick, and that the Dead House with a straw loft overhead could be built on. In December 1842 a request for a further loan of £700 to complete the workhouse was made, to be repaid in 20 annual installments of £35.

The outline of the building as it was when surveyed in 1877 shows a rectangular building with an extension on the back for the kitchen and some outbuildings, probably the infirmary, wash house and labour areas. The dining hall occupied the centre of the main building on the groundfloor, with the Master's room and boys and girls dayrooms (1855 drawing). The Boardroom was directly over the dining room with the male and female dormitories on either side and the attics for boys and girls above. In April 1842 the workhouse could accommodate 166.

| Rooms | No. of beds | No. of inmates |
|---|---|---|
| Women's Room | 12 beds | 24 people |
| Girls' | 14 | 28 |
| Boys' | 14 | 28 |
| Men's | 16 | 16 |
| Girls' Attic | 10 | 20 |
| Boys' | 10 | 20 |
| Male Infirmary | 7 | 7 |
| Female | 7 | 7 |
| | _____ | _____ |
| | 90 | 150 |
| Male Receiving Ward | | 8 |
| Female | | 8 |
| | | _____ |
| | | 166 |

In 1855 the accommodation for the Master and Matron was discussed
and a plan to make the dining room smaller and use the extra
space for a parlour for the Master and Matron was submitted to
the Board. Workhouse Inspector Doyle thought the change
unnecessary as the Master already had a sitting room on the
groundfloor. The Board thought the dining room would be too small
if divided, and refused the proposed alterations. Unfortunately
the alterations had already been made — it was a retrospective
application for permission. The dining room had to be re-enstated
to its original size, which suited the Guardians who had not

agreed with the alteration, and in the event of an increase in
the number of inmates, proved to be a good decision on the part
of the Board.

In 1867 Richard Cane, the Union Inspector, reported that the
Guardians were resolved to erect Male and Female sick wards and
improve the existing building. The Board agreed to the plans and
to £300 being borrowed from the Exchequer Bill Loan Commissioners
with repayment over 12 years. However,Thomas Drinkwater of Mellor
offered to lend £300 at 4% and the Board agreed to this
arrangement. Richard Cane wrote that the new wards would enhance
the workhouse.

In October the Guardians decided sheds were needed for the
able-bodied and vagrants to work in, picking oakum and breaking
stone. A shed 36 feet long, 12 feet wide and 10 feet high was to
be built and divided into three:- Stone shed 16.5 feet long

                              Oakum   "   16.5   "

                              Oakum store 3.0   "


In February,1868 Mr. Cane wrote that the new buildings were
partly completed and were built on the site of the old store
rooms. In July he reported "the detached hospital was complete as

were the work rooms". There were two lying-in beds, eight female
infirmary beds, four female fever beds, ten male infirmary beds
and three male fever beds. There was also a nurses room with
three beds. In January,1869 the figures given differed slightly
in the distribution but agreed in total.

In 1872 the Guardians decided to alter the existing Vagrant wards
and workrooms in order to adopt the separate cell system by which
vagrants slept in individual cells rather than in a dormitory.
The architectural notes detail the changes:

> Lengthen the existing vagrancy wards by approximately 15
> feet each and form in the building thus obtained 7 cells
> for men and 5 for women, a bathroom for each sex and a
> pump room. Each cell to be 10 feet by 3 feet by 10 feet
> high. 7 labour cells 9 feet by 4 feet with stone hoppers
> and also a receiving and fumigating room.

Such a block appears on plan 15046/96. By January,1873 the cells
ere reported to be in use.

In 1892 a letter from the L.G.B. stated sick accommodation and
isolation wards should be available. The existing female sick
ward should be taken down and the male block extended by some
50-60 feet, but in January,1896 the Guardians were still saying
that "if any alterations were planned" they would be in line with
the L.G.B.'s suggestions. The following meeting Mr. J.T.Gee
(Hayfield) asked if any land was available at the rear of the
existing workhouse which could be bought. In June,1896 Joseph
Hudson presented a plan for a new Boardroom which was accepted
and sent to the L.G.B. When Mr. Stephens (workhouse Inspector)
visited in August, he said alterations to the female sick wards

should be considered at the same time as those of the new
Boardroom. The Workhouse Committee said that the L.G.B.
suggestion of 1892 should be augmented and the existing Boardroom
should be converted into a Dayroom for female children, and the
children's Dayroom be made into one for the women, as their
dayroom was used as a laundry. A piece of land, belonging to the
Society of Friends, at the rear of the property, was for sale and
it was decided to open negotiations to buy it. Both the plan of
the land and the conveyance have survived. If the land was
bought, the Guardians would be required to divert the highway and
erect a boundary wall. Providing this was done, the Society of
Friends were happy to sell the land to the Guardians.

The diversion of the road was granted at the Quarter Sessions on
29th June 1898. In January 1899 the mortgage was arranged, £250
was borrowed at 3% over 30 years and the conveyance was signed on
26th January 1899 by Henry J.Whitehouse in the presence of the
Clerk, A.Walker.In June 1899, the L.G.B. accepted the latest
plans submitted and gave permission for the work to start .
However, in July, the Guardians decided to postpone the start of
the building , as a Select Committee Report on "Cottage Homes"
was due to be published. If a new way to house the poor and needy
was accepted and made law, the Guardians thought the extensions
would not be needed. The L.G.B. countered by saying that the
infirmary must be built and the improvements to the receiving
wards and the bathing facilities in the main building must be
carried out even if all else was abandoned. In January, 1900, the

Guardians compromised by offering to erect new female vagrant wards, convert the block of buildings containing the wash house into a proper laundry, erect a new oakum room and water closet elsewhere if required,and convert the new building into an infirmary and use the present sick wards for the able-bodied.The L.G.B. was not impressed, and during the year there was much correspondence, including a letter in September from the Guardians, saying that as everything was depressed,they could not afford £6,000,so they put off the work for twelve months. Kinder Print Works had closed in July,1900, and Calico Printing was on short time at Hayfield, Birch Vale and other villages. The L.G.B. agreed to leave any action until after the elections in 1901.

In April 1901, a new Board of Guardians was elected, and within two months plans were sent to the L.G.B., which were sanctioned in August and a loan of £5,345, over 30 years, and of £1,000 over 15 years, had been agreed to. The loan was granted at 3% by the Public Works Loan Commission on 6th February 1902. The alterations and buildings were not to exceed £6,345 and tenders were requested in December.

The actual plans used no longer exist, but the layout of the present buildings suggests that the plans of 1899 were the basis with a few alterations. The second storey of the infirmary of 1899 was not built,except fpr the nurses quarters over the porch. In January 1903 £1,000 was spent on furnishing the new premises including 21 hammocks for the casual wards and 56 ordinary iron

beds at 18/6 each(91p),2 epileptic beds at 18/6 each and 2
falling end beds at £1/5/6 (£1.26) each.

The final building at the workhouse was the new Boardroom. The
existing Boardroom was to be made into a bedroom and sitting room
for the Master and his existing bedroom was to be converted into
a bathroom and toilet. The Master's sitting room was to become a
waiting room/Committee room. The new Boardroom was to be a free
standing building in the back garden of the workhouse, facing
east and west,and would include a Committee room and waiting
room. The dining room would be used as a temporary Boardroom and
the existing porter's lodge and schoolroom could be a Dayroom.
The plan is lost but a very detailed description survives, as
does the building. The building was to be detached, the room 46
feet by 24 feet, with two flues and chimneystacks. There were to
be two bay windows, and the room was to be 17 feet in height. A
waiting room 14 feet square with radiators was included in the
price of £750. A loan at 3% from the Public Works Loan Committee
was obtained.A plaque,simply saying "Erected 1906" was placed on
the inside wall and the first meeting was held in the new room in
April 1907 by the retiring Guardians.

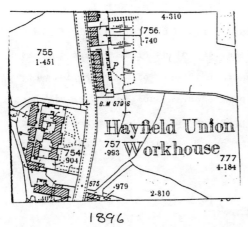

1896

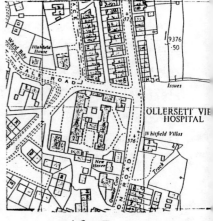

1967

# The Guardians

The highest level of society in the area covered by Hayfield
Union were landowners and large employers. The next level
consisted of tradesmen and farmers. It was from these groups that
the first Guardians were elected. At the first meeting on 7th
December 1837, there were 16 elected guardians, four for each of
the parishes of Hayfield,Mellor and Disley and one each for
Beard, Ollersett,Whitle and Thornsett.The qualification to stand
for election to the position was to hold property with a rental
of at least £30 per annum.This of course limited the number of
people able to stand for election, and because of the law of the
time, meant that all contestants were male. It was not until the
Local Government Act of 1894 that the property qualification and
plural voting were removed.Women became eligible to be guardians
in the 1880s. At Hayfield, when the new Board Room was being
planned, the L.G.B. suggested that a cloakroom for lady guardians
should be included,but the guardians declared that there would
never be any women guardians to use it! Justices of the Peace sat
on the Board ex officio, elections of guardians were annual until
1887 after which date they were held every three years.

The occupations of the Guardians reflected the predominance of
the Textile industry in the area. Of the first sixteen Guardians,
eight were connected with cotton or wool, three were listed as
Gentlemen, one was a Coalmaster,one a farmer and one a builder
and joiner.  The three Local J.P.s, John White of Parkhall,

Richard Simpson of Mellor Lodge and Moses Hadfield of Mellor completed the roll. From the start some of the Guardians took an on-going interest in the work of supervising the poor and setting the Poor Rate, and stood for election year after year. The Church also offered its ministers and vicars as Guardians, The Reverend S.Wasse represented Hayfield from 1842-46:Reverend C.J.Satherthwaite of Disley served from 1863-66 or67:Father McKenna of New Mills served many years from 1895. Reverend R.R.Ricketts represented Hayfield at the same time as Father McKenna,and Father Prendergast served 1927-30 as New Mills Guardian.

In 1841 the number of Guardians for Beard,Ollersett, Whitle and Thornsett was increase to five. As the district's population grew, the number of Guardians increased until a final number of twenty was reached. At first meetings were weekly, then after many years were held fortnightly and eventually once each month.

## TABLE I

### Occupations of Guardians

| Occupation | 1847 | 1858 | 1865 | 1878 | 1879 |
|---|---|---|---|---|---|
| Calico printing | 8 | | | | |
| Cotton | | 4 | 8 | | |
| Farming | 4 | 4 | 3 | 4 | 4 |
| Innkeeper | 2 | 2 | | 1 | |
| Vicar | 1 | | 1 | | |
| Builder | | 2 | 1 | | |
| Bleacher | | 1 | 1 | 2 | 1 |
| Shopkeeper | 1 | | | | |
| Butcher | | 1 | | | |
| Gentleman | | | | 3 | 2 |
| Coal Prprietor | 1 | 1 | 1 | 2 | 2 |
| Commission Agent | | | | 2 | |
| Draper | | | | 1 | 2 |
| Paper Manufacturer | | | | 1 | |
| Dry Salter | | | | | 1 |
| Agent | | | | | 1 |
| Yoeman | | | | | 1 |
| Candler | | | | | 1 |
| Manufacturing Chemist | | | | | 1 |

The post of Guardian was not always popular and it could be very time consuming especially in the early years of weekly meetings. It has not been thought necessary to record the attendences of the Guardians for every year,but samples taken from four years show that most Guardians took their responsibilities seriously by attending regularly, often in spite of being busy businessmen. While some only served for one term of office,many served for long periods. J.T.Gee of Hayfield is recorded as a Guardian in 1887, and continued to act as such until his death in 1916. J.Jowett of Disley served for nearly twenty years.

As the Local Government Board tried to remove the stigma from the term "workhouse",the Guardians appear to have become more liberal in their attitudes to the inmates. Their wives also became more interested and began to dispense their charity to the workhouse inmates as well as the poor at home. In 1897 it was recorded in the Minutes that Mrs. Wilson had given tobacco and tea, Mrs. Mason had provided 28 buns and Mrs. Mackie had given shoulder shawls and scarves. Magazines and periodicals were also donated at various times,including the Tatler and the London Illustrated News. What the inmates thought of them is not recorded!
The Guardians showed more thought for the diet of the inmates,not so much to change it ,but as regards its presentation, especially for older and sick inmates.Thickness of bread and uneatable food were commented upon and steps taken to improve both. A bread slicer was purchased to stop thick hunks being given out and the House Committee recommended that the Medical Officer should be

able to prescribe eggs and other delicacies such as beef tea and cocoa for the sick. Extra blankets were provided by "a lady", and a wagonette provided by Mr. Ricketts took inmates on an outing at the Queen's Diamond Jubilee.A subscription Tea and coffee, cheese and tobacco were also provided.

## TABLE II

### Attendances of Guardians

| 1845-48 Max 52 | | 1877-78 Max 26 | | 1887-88 Max 26 | | 1929-30 Max 15 | |
|---|---|---|---|---|---|---|---|
| J.Yates | 9 | W.Taylor | 26 | J.Fielding | 23 | R.Moreton | 10 |
| J.Thorpe | 33 | J.Fielding | 22 | J.Hibbert | 16 | S.Evans | 10 |
| J.Bennett | 20 | J.Wood | 16 | Winterbottom | 18 | J.W.Cochrane | 3 |
| Ja. Yates | 5 | A.Mellor | 21 | Chambers | 26 | W.B.Farmer | 14 |
| G.Woolley | 11 | J.T.Gee | 15 | Tollerens | 1 | W.Bowden | 10 |
| A.Vickers | 18 | T.Bowden | 21 | J.A.Bennett | 14 | W.A.Collins | 15 |
| L.Slater | 25 | W.R.Moore | 9 | T.Drinkwater | 23 | A.E.Gwilt | 13 |
| W.Travis | 25 | J.Jowett | 19 | P.Wild | 25 | J.S.Beaumont | 6 |
| J.Dixon | 35 | G.Cook | 18 | S.Bullock | 11 | G.Jennison | 10 |
| S.Wasse | 20 | J.Wild | 3 | J.Wood | 12 | B.Whitehead | 12 |
| J.Bowden | 17 | J.Cooper | 23 | J.Hibbert | 15 | W.Drinkwater | 10 |
| G.Redfern | 16 | J.Goddard | 19 | J.T.Gee | 24 | G.Griffiths | 13 |
| J.Hurst | 18 | J.Grundy | 21 | Atherton | 12 | A.J.Larkum | 13 |
| J.Jowett | 19 | G.Smith | 19 | Cooper | 15 | G.H.Eastwood | 11 |
| J.Moult | 23 | Latham | 4 | Walton | 9 | J.W.Sutton | 6 |
| J.Arnfield | 12 | W.F.Hill | 6 | Jowett | 9 | H.Wood | 14 |

The Guardians on the whole did try to care for the poor and needy
to the best of their ability, but as business men they also tried
to keep the Poor Rate as low as possible. Their tardiness in
replacing out of date buildings, and procrastination in providing
better sick care is revealed in the Minute Books and the
Correspondence files between 1890 and 1903 when plans were
forever being drawn up but were followed by reasons why they
should not be built.

# The Masters

Instructions given to the overseers and churchwardens in Kendal
by the Rev. W.D.Crewdson, influenced the instructions drawn up
for the Master of Kendal Workhouse.(18)

> "Your duties are... to reform the dissolute, to arouse
> the idle, to punish the refractory, to be in place of
> father to the orphan, husband to the widow, to smooth
> the path of declining age....dependence ought never to be
> placed on servants..in you..it rests to encourage the well
> behaved and orderly poor so as to return them to society
> again with spirit as little broken by requiring and
> receiving this parochial aid, as circumstances permit."

Masters or matrons were not expected to have any specific
qualifications or experience, and received no on-job training.
Sometimes a military background-retired sargeant major- was
considered as suitable previous experience for the ideal master.
Andover chose such a man and his wife as its master and matron
and the result was the "Scandal of the Andover Workhouse", which
was partly responsible for the replacement of the P.L.C. by the
P.L.B. in 1847.One master was reported as having stolen the
pauper's rations and run the place as a penal settlement rather
than an asylum for the poor and needy(19).Usually the posts of
master and matron were filled by a man and wife (20) and they had
complete juristriction over adults and children and sick and

able-bodied.The master decided on how much deterrance should be used,but the guardians were meant to ensure that matters did not get out of hand. When guardians did not supervise properly, a bad master could make life unbearable for the inmates, as happened at Andover.(21) At Southwell a master tied a log to the leg of a mentally deficient woman who kept running away(22). Another master was found to have been drinking the brandy, wine, gin and ale kept for medicinal purposes in the workhouse.A couple at Milnthorpe workhouse were dismissed after the death of an inmate, accused of disregard of the discomfort of the deceased, internment without notice of enquiry and want of common decency and kindness. Although there were much publicised cases of cruel masters and matrons,out of the ten couples who held the posts in Hayfield Union only one couple were dismissed as being bad at their jobs.(23)

If the master died the matron could continue until the end of the quarter and then had to resign. At Hayfield two masters died while still serving, and in one case his widow was allowed to continue and the Relieving officer acted as master by special dispensation after an appeal from the guardians. In the second case the master's daughter, who had taken over as matron on the death of her mother, was to be allowed to continue but actually resigned after she and the nurse were accused of illtreating an inmate.(24)Guardians did tend to believe the master's story rather than that of inmates, and at Hayfield inmates complained of a master and matron for four years before the L.G.B. finally demanded that the master and matron resigned(25).

PRO
MH12 2041 16715/1
46

RECEIVED P.L.C. OCT 11 1844

# HAYFIELD UNION.

Extract from the Quarterly Abstract, showing the Number of Paupers relieved, the amount of Money expended, and the Balances due to and from the several Townships, for the Quarter ending 25th day

Form 11.d.

**TOTALS.**

| TOWNSHIPS. | In-door. Adults. Males. | In-door. Adults. Females. | In-door. Children. | Out-door. Adults. Males. | Out-door. Adults. Females. | Out-door. Children. | GRAND TOTAL. |
|---|---|---|---|---|---|---|---|
| Hayfield.......... | 4 | 6 | 12 | 14 | 27 | 37 | 100 |
| Beard, Ollerset, Whitle & Thornset | 6 | 5 | 11 | 31 | 58 | 48 | 159 |
| .......... | 5 | 4 | 5 | 11 | 30 | 23 | 78 |
| .......... | .. | 4 | 6 | 10 | 18 | 17 | 55 |
| TOTAL... | 15 | 19 | 34 | 66 | 133 | 125 | 392 |
| Increase... | .. | .. | .. | .. | .. | .. | ...... |
| Diminution. | 16 | 1 | 9 | 16 | 22 | 71 | 135 |

**EXPENDITURE.**

| TOWNSHIPS. | Repayment of Workhouse and Emigration Loans. £ | s. | d. | Amount of Relief advanced by way of Loans, under 58th, and 59th, Sections of Poor Law Amendment Act. £ | s. | d. | Proportion of In-Maintenance. £ | s. | d. | Out-Relief. £ | s. | £ | Proportion of Establishment Charges. £ | s. | d. |
|---|---|---|---|---|---|---|---|---|---|---|---|---|---|---|---|
| Hayfield | .. | .. | .. | .. | .. | .. | 18 | 17 | 9 | 55 | 0 | 2¾ | 24 | 9 | 4½ |
| Beard, Ollerset, Whitle & Thornset | .. | .. | .. | .. | .. | .. | 21 | 2 | 8¼ | 117 | 16 | 2¼ | 41 | 14 | 10½ |
| .......... | .. | .. | .. | .. | .. | .. | 15 | 9 | 2¼ | 52 | 7 | 0 | 13 | 17 | 1¼ |
| .......... | .. | .. | .. | .. | .. | .. | 9 | 7 | 9½ | 41 | 12 | 2 | 15 | 15 | 3 |
| TOTAL | .. | .. | .. | .. | .. | .. | 64 | 17 | 5 | 266 | 15 | 7 | 95 | 16 | 7½ |
| Increase | .. | .. | .. | .. | .. | .. | 0 | 13 | 4¼ | 3 | 7 | 5¼ | .. | .. | .. |
| Diminution | .. | .. | .. | .. | .. | .. | .. | .. | .. | .. | .. | .. | 58 | 11 | 5¾ |

| TOWNSHIPS. | Total Expenditure for the Relief of the Poor. £ | s. | d. | Registrating Fees. £ | s. | d. | £ | s. | d. | Total Expenditure, including Relief to the Poor and Registrating Expenses. £ | s. | d. |
|---|---|---|---|---|---|---|---|---|---|---|---|---|
| Hayfield | 98 | 7 | 4¼ | 2 | 5 | 6 | .. | .. | .. | 100 | 12 | 10¼ |
| Beard, Ollerset, Whitle & Thornset | 180 | 13 | 9 | 5 | 13 | 0 | .. | .. | .. | 186 | 6 | 9 |
| .......... | 81 | 13 | 3¾ | 1 | 17 | 7½ | .. | .. | .. | 83 | 10 | 11¼ |
| .......... | 66 | 15 | 2½ | 2 | 11 | 10½ | .. | .. | .. | 69 | 7 | 1 |
| TOTAL | 427 | 9 | 7½ | 12 | 8 | 0 | .. | .. | .. | 439 | 17 | 7½ |
| Increase | .. | .. | .. | 5 | 0 | 0 | .. | .. | .. | .. | .. | .. |
| Diminution | 55 | 17 | 4½ | .. | .. | .. | .. | .. | .. | 50 | 8 | 4½ |

| TOWNSHIPS. | Balance due to the Township. £ | s. | d. | Balance due from the Township. £ | s. | d. | Comparison of the corresponding Quarter last year: PAUPERS. In-door. Increase. | In-door. Decrease. | Out-door. Increase. | Out-door. Decrease. | EXPENDITURE. Increase. £ | s. | d. | Decrease. £ | s. |
|---|---|---|---|---|---|---|---|---|---|---|---|---|---|---|---|
| Hayfield | 60 | 2 | 4 | .. | .. | .. | 2 | .. | .. | 24 | .. | .. | .. | 15 | 13 |
| Beard, Ollerset, Whitle & Thornset | .. | .. | .. | 21 | 2 | 6 | .. | 27 | .. | 37 | .. | .. | .. | 12 | 9 |
| .......... | .. | .. | .. | 30 | 0 | 9½ | .. | .. | .. | 17 | .. | .. | .. | 11 | 19 |
| .......... | 67 | 9 | 2¾ | .. | .. | .. | .. | 1 | .. | 31 | .. | .. | .. | 10 | 6 |
| TOTAL | 127 | 11 | 6¾ | 51 | 3 | 3½ | 2 | 28 | .. | 109 | .. | .. | .. | 50 | 8 |
| Increase | .. | .. | .. | 51 | 3 | 3½ | .. | .. | .. | .. | .. | .. | .. | .. | .. |
| Diminution | 78 | 18 | 11¾ | .. | .. | .. | [illegible] | 26 | .. | 109 | .. | .. | .. | .. | .. |

EBEN. ADAMSON

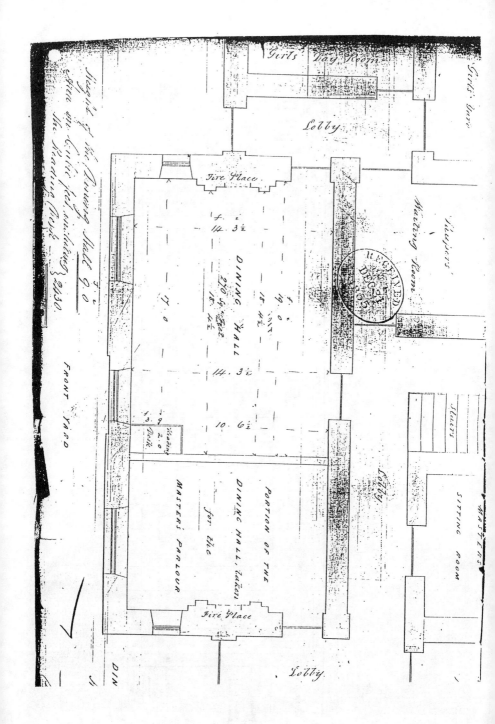

A Front centre block of work house showing Dining room on groundfloor;boardroom on first floor and children's attics 1841
B Male reception block on right with vagrant block in background 1903.
C Boy's or girl's attic 1841
D Steps down to cellar of 1841 building
E Slate bath under stairs in cellar of 1841 building
F Bench and window in cellar
G Vagrant cell in 1903 Vagrant block

F

G

39055/56

Mayfield Union.

At a Meeting of the Board of Guardians of the Mayfield Union, held on the 13th day of October 1856, it was Resolved that the following Dietary Tables for the Pauper Children from 2 to 9 years of age, hereunder described in the Workhouse of the said Union, be submitted for the sanction and approval of the Poor Law Board.

RECEIVED P.L.B. OCT 18 1856

TABLE A.

Children from 2 to 5.

| | BREAKFAST | | DINNER | | | | | | SUPPER | | |
|---|---|---|---|---|---|---|---|---|---|---|---|
| | Bread | Milk Porridge | Meat | Bread | Potatoes | Pea Soup | Potatoe & Meat Hash | Suet Pudding | Bread | Milk | Meal Porridge |
| | oz | pts | oz | oz | oz | pts | oz | oz | oz | pts | lb |
| Sunday .. .. .. | 3 | 1 | 2 | 2 | 8 | . | . | . | 4 | ½ | . |
| Monday .. .. .. | 3 | 1 | . | 3 | . | 1 | . | . | 4 | ½ | . |
| Tuesday .. .. .. | 3 | 1 | . | 2 | . | . | 14 | . | 4 | ½ | . |
| Wednesday .. .. | 3 | 1 | 2 | 2 | 8 | . | . | . | 4 | ½ | . |
| Thursday .. .. | 3 | 1 | . | 3 | . | 1 | . | . | 4 | ½ | . |
| Friday .. .. .. | 3 | 1 | | 2 | . | . | 14 | . | 4 | ½ | . |
| Saturday .. .. | 3 | 1 | . | . | . | . | . | 8 | 4 | ½ | . |

TABLE B.

Children from 5 to 9.

| | BREAKFAST | | DINNER | | | | | | SUPPER | | |
|---|---|---|---|---|---|---|---|---|---|---|---|
| | Bread | Milk Porridge | Meat | Bread | Potatoes | Pea Soup | Potatoe & Meat Hash | Suet Pudding | Bread | Milk | Meal Porridge |
| | oz | pts | oz | oz | oz | pts | oz | oz | oz | pts | lb |
| Sunday .. .. .. | 4 | 1 | 3 | 2 | 10 | . | . | . | 5 | ½ | . |
| Monday .. .. .. | 4 | 1 | . | 3 | . | 1 | . | . | . | ½ | 1 |
| Tuesday .. .. .. | 4 | 1 | . | 2 | . | . | 16 | . | . | ½ | 1 |
| Wednesday .. .. | 4 | 1 | 3 | 2 | 10 | . | . | . | . | ½ | 1 |
| Thursday .. .. | 4 | 1 | . | 3 | . | 1 | . | . | . | ½ | 1 |
| Friday .. .. .. | 4 | 1 | . | 2 | . | . | 16 | . | . | ½ | 1 |
| Saturday .. .. | 4 | 1 | . | . | . | . | . | 12 | . | ½ | 1 |

Children under 2 years of age to be dieted at discretion.

William Taylor *Presiding Chairman.*

I consider the allowances in the above Dietaries to be sufficient.

T. R. Jackson *Medical Officer.*

The Poor Law Board sanction the above Dietary Tables.

*Poor Law Board,*

185

______________ *Secretary.*

753 3|56—H & S 3440

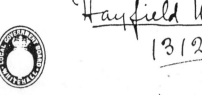

Hayfield Union
131250
98

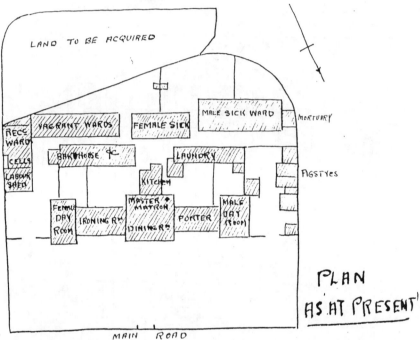

LAND TO BE ACQUIRED

VAGRANT WARDS · FEMALE SICK · MALE SICK WARD · MORTUARY

RECS WARD
CELLS
LABOUR SHED
BAKEHOUSE &c
LAUNDRY
PIGSTYES

KITCHEN

FEMALE DAY ROOM · IRONING Rm · MASTER & MATRON · DINING Rm · PORTER · MALE DAY (ROOM)

MAIN ROAD

**PLAN
AS AT PRESENT**

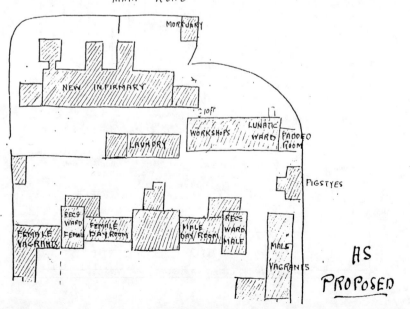

MORTUARY

NEW INFIRMARY

10 ft

WORKSHOPS · LUNATIC WARD · PADDED ROOM

LAUNDRY

PIGSTYES

FEMALE VAGRANTS · RECS WARD FEMALE · FEMALE DAY ROOM · MALE DAY ROOM · RECS WARD MALE · MALE VAGRANTS

**AS
PROPOSED**

## Table III

### Masters and Matrons at Hayfield Union

| Name | Tenure | Age | Salary | Previous Occupation |
|------|--------|-----|--------|---------------------|
| 1.John Slater | 1841-47 | 46 | £40 | Bleacher/Master |
| Elizabeth | | 40 | 36 | |
| 2.John Ratcliffe | 1847-51 | 40 | 25 | Shopkeeper |
| Hannah | | 30 | 15 | |
| 3.Job Harrison | 1851-58 | 35 | 60 | Asylum Steward |
| Betty | | 35 | 20 | |
| 4.William Wyatt | 1858-63 | 34 | 25 | Powerloom overlooker |
| Elizabeth | | 34 | 15 | |
| 5.Samuel Simpson | 1863-69 | | 24-35 | |
| Harriet | | | 16-24 | |
| 6.John Waterhouse | 1869-79 | 63 | 20 | Relieving Officer |
| Harriet Simpson | | | 30 | |
| 7.John Livesley | 1879-97 | 47 | 30 | |
| Harriet | 79-91 | | 20 | |
| Martha Ann | 91-97 | | 20 | |
| 8.George Fairfax | 1 month | 40 | | Asylum Attendent |
| Martha Ann Levesley | | 24 | | |
| 9.Henry Savage | 1897-1903 | 37 | 35 | Soldier/Master |
| Elizabeth | | 37 | 25 | Nurse/Matron |
| 10 Mr. Reynolds | 1903-30 | | 35 | Porter |
| Mrs. Reynolds | | | 25 | Porteress |

The Master and Matron were also entitled to rations to the value of £36 per year for the two of them and free accommodation.

In the 89 years that Hayfield Union Workhouse existed there were
ten masters. The first John Slater had been dismissed as Master
at Salford for "lack of humility". Charles Lucas, a Hayfield
Guardian and Calico Printer,had known Slater as a Bleacher, and
recommended him as "good with accounts". He said the lack of
humility was the result of celebrating the Queen's birthday too
well and upsetting the Guardians on his return. He proved a good
Master and on the resignation of Ebebezer Adamson in 1847,he
resigned as Master and became Clerk to the Guardians.

The second master, John Ratcliffe, was asked to resign after he
had been absent for eight days and "neglected his duties".With
the agreement of the Poor Law Inspector Andrew Doyle, the
Guardians asked the P.L.B. if the jobs of master and relieving
officer could be combined. Permission was given and Job Harrison
took on the two jobs at a total salary of £60 with his wife
receiving £20 as Matron,for a trial period of six months which
then became permanent.In Decmeber 1857 Samuel Frith accused the
Master of hitting him when he came for relief. The Guardians took
the Master's word that it was a lie and dismissed the case.
However Harrison went before the Magistrates and was fined 20/-
and expenses of £2/2/3 which the Guardians paid! The P.L.B. wrote
asking for an explanation after receiving a letter from the Clerk
to the Justices, and in spite of the Guardians explanation
decided that the two jobs should be separated. Mr. Harrison

resigned as Master but continued as Relieving Officer for another year before resigning to become Master at Ashton-under-Lyne.

The fifth Master, Samuel Simpson and his wife, had their salaries increased within six months because they took on the servants work when she left. Simpson died suddenly and according to Article 180 of the General Consolidated Order (26), Mrs. Simpson should have left at the end of the quarter. The Guardians asked that she be allowed to continue as Matron and that the Relieving Officer should also act as Master. The P.L.B. agreed as the union was a small one and the Relieving Officer could get around easily on foot or by train, and he had run the two jobs for two months sucessfully. Mrs. Simpson's salary was increased to £30 as she would have more responsibility and the fee for the combined job was £80. In 1879 Mr. Harrison fell when in Hayfield and damaged his foot. He was then aged 73, and as his foot did not improve he resigned as did Mrs. Simpson in spite of entreaties from the Guardians.

The seventh Master's appointment was rather contraversial. The advertisement stated that"there should be no encumbrances", yet the Livesley's had a six year old daughter. They were charged 3/- per week out of their salaries for twelve months to see how they managed. It worked out well. Mr. Livesley's two brothers lived in New Mills, one a butcher, the other a chemist.In 1884 when the Relieving Officer died, Mr. Livesley offered to do the two jobs but the Local Government Boeard refused.Mrs. Livesley died in

1890 and her daughter Marthe Ann aged 18 took over as Matron. Mr. Livesley could be a hard taskmaster,and was criticised by Father McKenna, Guardian for New Mills, who said "this is not a prison but an asylum for the poor and needy and no one should be "taxed" to this extent". A man had been refused a lunch because Mr. Livesley said he had worked three minute less than the two hours stipulated to receive a lunch. Another Guardian complained on behalf of patients in sick wards who were given fat bacon and cold potaotes which they coundn't eat, and thick hunks of bread which they couldn't chew. In his defense Mr. Livesley said he did not have enough butter to go around if the bread was cut thinly. The Guardians ordered a breadslicer but there is no record of an increase in the amount of butter purchased. Before any further action was taken, Mr.Livesley died on the 24th May 1897. Once more the Guardians asked that the Matron be allowed to continue in her office and a single man be taken on as Master. The L.G.B. agreed providing" the man was over 40 years of age. at a salary of £35 per annum plus rations, laundry and appartment". George Fairfax only held the position for a month as his age was queried by a Guardian and the only evidence he could produce of his age was the "his mother had told him".Miss Livesley also resigned following newspaper reports that the the workhouse nurse had"slapped women, whipped a baby to stop it crying, tied a girl's hands to a chair and hit Mrs. Marriott"((27)

The ninth Master and his wife actually had qualifications,or at least experience,which should have made them suitable for the job,but almost from the first there was trouble. During their service (six Years) five nurses were appointed and resigned, the Matron saying the nurses were not suitable, the nurses saying that the Matron interferred too much. The Master complained about the amount of space he had in the workhouse and the inmates clothing. He was cautioned for not keeping the "Spirit Book" properly, and the Guardians complained to him about the waste of food because it was not cooked properly. The Master tried to stop the inmates sitting in the yards or gardens,to which the Guardians replied" this is an almshouse not a prison". Bickering between the Guardians and the Master resulted in the L.G.B. asking for the suspension of the Master in June 1901 and the Relieving Officer,Thomas Mower was appointed to act as Master pro tem. The Guardians found the books were not kept properly, that inmates were forced to wash clothes on Sundays,short measures were given of alcohol for medicinal purposes and Mr. Savage was threatening and abusive. An enquiry was ordered by the L.G.B. which resulted in the Savages' resignation in January 1902.

The final and longest serving Master was Mr. Reynolds. He started in 1903 at a salary of £35 which was raised in 1907 to £40. With the building of the new Boardroom his quarters were enlarged and refurbished. In July 1917 he put up the "closed" sign on the vagrant wards due to the fall in the numbers of Casuals needing a bed for the night. The Guardians voted a gratuity of £25 to be paid that year to be paid towards the cost of the Matron's operation. In 1927 the Master was ill for six months and a grant operation. In 1927 the Master was ill for six months and a grant of £40 was divided between the members of the staff who had done his work during that time. In 1930 the Master was ill again and the Porter deputised for him. The last Master and staff joined the Guardians in a farewell dinner at the Hare and Hounds, Low Leighton on the 27th March 1930 and the workhouse closed its doors for the 1st time.

# The Inmates

The admission of paupers to a workhouse was strictly laid down by
the Commissioners. The prospective inmate had to be formally
accepted by the Master with a written order, in a Reception ward.
Here he,or she, was examined by the Medical Officer and if sick,
sent to the appropriate sick ward. If not sick, the pauper was
sent to the part of the workhouse where his,or her, class was
located. There were seven classes in the workhouse:-

1.  Old and/or infirm men

2.  Able-bodied men and youths over the age of 15

3.  Boys between  7 and 15 years

4.  Old and/or infirm women

5.  Able-bodied women and girls over the age of 15

6.  Girls between 7 and 15

7.  Children under 7 years of age (28)

Each" class" had a specific area in the workhouse and was not
expected to mix with any other "class". Women and girls were
expected to help in the female sick wards,care for babies and
help with the housework. Able-bodied women were also expected to
"crush stone" for two hours a day. Able-bodied men and youths had
to do any work ordered by the Master or Guardians, including
picking oakum and stone breaking. Getting up, working, eating,and
going to bed were governed by the times ordered by the
Commissioners, and a roll call was made each morning, "each

31

pauper answering to their name". The Master was allowed to punish inmates for minor rudeness,insolence or misdemeanor

The diet for inmates was also strictly laid down. Over the years these dietary tables were reviewed and slightly altered, but the food was stodgey and monotonous, low in meat, fish, fresh fruit and vegetables and high in oatmeal,bread and potatoes. Breakfast in 1841 regularly consisted of two pounds of oatmeal, Monday to Saturday, with six ounces of bread and one and a half pints of milk porridge on Sunday. Supper was the same as breakfast Monday to Saturday, with six ounces of bread and two ounces of cheese on Sunday. Dinner did vary a little more, Monday and Thursday was six and a half ounces of bread and one and a half pints of pea soup,Friday and Saturday three ounces of bread and two pounds of hash, and Wednesday and Sunday, five ounces of meat and two pounds of potatoes. By 1897 the diet was a little more varied in that milk porrage was served for breakfast instead of oatmeal, but supper still had oatmeal although milk was added to the meal on weekdays while tea or coffee was available on Sundays. Potato pies, suet pudding and rice or sago pudding were added to the dinner menus. The diet ensured that the paupers did not starve, but was designed to fill them up in the cheapest manner, and was possibly better than some had outside the workhouse. Christmas dinner and tea were the highlights of those early years, with Roast beef and Plum pudding and currant bread, but as the century progressed "treats" became more frequent and currant bread was served for Sunday supper, and gifts of tobacco and tea were distributed at Christmas and national celebrations.

An analysis of the census enumerator's books (1851-1891) provides more detail on the inmates occupations and birthplaces, their ages, sex and sometimes their mental or physical disabilities, Ages ranged from birth to over eighty and were fairly evenly divided between male and female. Children tended to be with their mothers, although in 1861 "a lost child about one year old, birthplace unknown" was listed. The majority of those aged 60 and over tended to be widowed or unmarried and had become inmates possibly because they were no longer able to look after themselves. The former occupations of the inmates indicate a strong connection with the cotton or calico printing industries, the largest employers in the area, closely followed by agriculture.

Table IV

Inmates listed by Sex

| Year | Male | Female | Total |
|------|------|--------|-------|
| 1851 | 16 | 14 | 30 |
| 1861 | 21 | 16 | 37 |
| 1871 | 26 | 23 | 49 |
| 1881 | 49 | 29 | 78 |
| 1891 | 27 | 15 | 47 |

Table V

Inmates listed by Sex and Age

| Age | 1851 | | 1861 | | 1871 | | 1881 | | 1891 | |
| --- | --- | --- | --- | --- | --- | --- | --- | --- | --- | --- |
| | M | F | M | F | M | F | M | F | M | F |
| 1–10 | 3 | 3 | 3 | 2 | 7 | 5 | 11 | 8 | 0 | 0 |
| 11–20 | 4 | 0 | 2 | 2 | 2 | 2 | 3 | 3 | 2 | 2 |
| 21–30 | 1 | 2 | 3 | 1 | 0 | 1 | 4 | 2 | 0 | 1 |
| 31–40 | 0 | 2 | 0 | 3 | 2 | 5 | 6 | 0 | 4 | 0 |
| 41–50 | 2 | 3 | 1 | 0 | 2 | 3 | 4 | 4 | 3 | 3 |
| 51–60 | 3 | 1 | 0 | 3 | 3 | 4 | 2 | 3 | 4 | 0 |
| 61–70 | 1 | 2 | 8 | 4 | 4 | 2 | 9 | 3 | 8 | 4 |
| 71–80 | 1 | 0 | 4 | 2 | 4 | 1 | 9 | 3 | 6 | 4 |
| over 80 | 1 | 1 | 0 | 0 | 1 | 0 | 1 | 0 | 0 | 1 |

The percentage of males and females aged 51–80 in 1851 was 37.5 per cent and 28.6 per cent respectively, showing that youth predominated amongst the inmates. In 1861 however, 57 per cent of males and 56.25 per cent of females were in the older age bracket suggesting that the under 50s were in work and not ill. The censuses of 1871 and 1881 showed averages of 44,5 per cent of males and 30.7 per cent of females were over 51, showing again that there was a larger number of younger people in the workhouse. In 1891, the last census available in detail, the majority of inmates were once more over 51 years of age.

Children were not to be found in large numbers in the workhouse at any time in the workhouse's existence,and it was perhaps for this reason that, after the first few years, the Guardians decided to send the children to the local National School rather than employ a teacher to teach the children within the workhouse. Children were usually accompanied by their parent or parents in the workhouse, but occasionally there were children on their own.

Table VI

Children in the Workhouse

| Year | Age | Unaccompanied | | With Family | |
|------|------|------|--------|------|--------|
|      |      | Male | Female | Male | Female |
| 1851 | 1-10 | 0 | 1 | 3 | 2 |
|      | 11-14 | 1 | 0 | 0 | 0 |
| 1861 | 1-10 | 3 | 2 | 1 | 0 |
|      | 11-14 | 2 | 0 | 1 | 0 |
| 1871 | 1-10 | 2 | 1 | 5 | 5 |
|      | 11-14 | 1 | 0 | 0 | 0 |
| 1881 | 1-10 | 0 | 2 | 11 | 6 |
|      | 11-14 | 1 | 0 | 1 | 0 |
| 1891 | 1-10 | 0 | 0 | 0 | 0 |
|      | 11-14 | 0 | 0 | 0 | 1 |

In January 1843 Edward Bradbury was appointed as teacher to the workhouse children at a salary of £5 per annum plus board and lodging. In June 1845 there were rumours that he "had taken improper liberties" with a young girl, and after investigation he was dismissed. In August 1845 Miss Slater, the 17 year old daughter of the Master was appointed as schoolmistress on a three month trial at a salary of £10 per annum plus rations. After the trial period, the position was made permanent. In December 1848 the Board was recorded as considering whether to appoint a school master or schoolmistress, but policy changed in the new year and it was decided to send the children to the National or church schools in the neighbourhood. In November, 1849 the inspector mentioned in his report that "the children were no longer taught in the workhouse but attended schools in the area". It is not known how many children were in the workhouse between 1843 and 1850, but the numbers recorded in the censuses were not large,so it can be assumed that in earlier years the situation had been the same.

In the tradesmen's bills for June-September 1861, James Whitehead,Schoolmaster, was paid £1/4/8. No record shows what service he was providing or at which school he taught. In September,1862,it was minuted that"a room should be provided for women to sew in and children sent to school". The accounts for December 1883 listed     "School fees for Pauper children" at the following schools:-

| | | | |
|---|---|---|---|
| Hayfield National | 8/6d | | |
| Hayfield Wesleyan | 5/9 | New Mills Board | 19/11 |
| New Mills National | 8/9 | Furness Vale School | 9/- |
| St. Mary's New Mills | 6/- | Mellor School | 15/9 |
| Thornsett Board | 16/5 | Newtown | 4/9 |

There is no reference as to whether these children were inmates or outdoor relief but it may be assumed to be a mixture from the number of schools mentioned.

Table VII

Children resident in the Workhouse 1851-1891

| Year | Age | Sex | | Total |
|---|---|---|---|---|
| | | Male | Female | |
| 1851 | 1-10 | 3 | 3 | |
| | 11-14 | 1 | 0 | 7 |
| 1861 | 1-10 | 4 | 2 | |
| | 11-14 | 3 | 0 | 9 |
| 1871 | 1-10 | 7 | 6 | |
| | 11-14 | 1 | 0 | 14 |
| 1881 | 1-10 | 11 | 8 | |
| | 11-14 | 1 | 0 | 20 |
| 1891 | 1-10 | 0 | 0 | |
| | 11-14 | 0 | 1 | 1 |

The regional lunatic asylum at Macclesfield was used to house mentally ill paupers, but some listed as "imbecile" or "idiot from childhood" were resident in the workhouse. Disabilities, such as blind, deaf, or dumb were shown in the Enumerator's returns and were differentiated as to whether the person was born with the disability or it came on in later life.The name and status of one "deaf and dumb"woman appears in the censuses for 1861, 1871 and 1891, and the *age increases correctly, so it would appear that this person was as inmate for at least 30 years.*

37

## Table VIII

### Former Occupations of inmates 1851–1891

|  | 1851 | 1861 | 1871 | 1881 | 1891 |
|---|---|---|---|---|---|
| Cotton | 13 | 5 | 14 | 15 | 10 |
| Calico Print | 1 | 0 | 7 | 14 | 6 |
| Farm Servant | 0 | 5 | 3 | 6 | 1 |
| Domestic " | 0 | 0 | 2 | 3 | 0 |
| Coal | 1 | 1 | 2 | 2 | 4 |
| Paper | 0 | 0 | 2 | 2 | 1 |
| Wool | 1 | 0 | 0 | 0 | 0 |
| Farmer | 1 | 0 | 0 | 0 | 0 |
| Mill Worker | 1 | 0 | 0 | 0 | 2 |
| Stone Mason | 1 | 0 | 1 | 0 | 0 |
| Joiner | 1 | 0 | 0 | 0 | 0 |
| Labourer | 3 | 0 | 0 | 4 | 3 |
| Brick maker | 0 | 0 | 0 | 1 | 1 |
| Boatman | 0 | 0 | 0 | 2 | 0 |
| Tailor | 0 | 0 | 0 | 1 | 0 |
| Assistant Surgeon | 0 | 0 | 0 | 1 | 1 |
| Rag Collector | 0 | 0 | 0 | 1 | 0 |
| Gardener | 0 | 0 | 0 | 1 | 0 |
| Milliner | 0 | 0 | 0 | 1 | 0 |
| Dressmaker | 0 | 0 | 0 | 0 | 2 |
| Blacksmith's Striker | 0 | 0 | 0 | 1 | 0 |

The main employment in the area was connected with cotton and
calico printing, with agriculture being the next biggest
employer. Periods of depression were regularly experienced in the
second half of the nineteenth century, and much short time and
unemployment were the result. For this reason it is not
surprising to find many ex-cotton workers in the workhouse as
they had not been able to build up any savings. In each of the
census years, the largest group in the workhouse was from the
cotton industry,only in 1861 was it in single figures. Calico
printing, while in second place, only equalled figures for cotton
in 1881. There were no calico printers in the workhouse in 1861,
only 1 in 1851 and 6 and 6 respectively in 1871 and 1891. The
highest number of agricultural workers in the workhouse occurred
in 1861 and 1881, otherwise the figures were between 0 and 3.

## Birthplace of Inmates

The place of birth of the inmates was varied. As immigration was
an important factor in the growth of the area in the nineteenth
century it was not surprising to find this showed up in the
birthplace of workhouse inmates. People born in Hayfield,
Ollersett and Thornsett and later became inmates formed 8.5% of
the inmates over the five census years,whereas those born in
Disley and Mellor were 21%. New Mills was the birthplace of 9.5%
of inmates in 1861-1891 census returns and the County of
Derbyshire provided 9%. The remainder of inmates were born
further afield in Lancashire(10.5%), Cheshire (6.5%), Scotland

(2%), Ireland(8%) and London(3.5%)

It is quite possible that some people preferred to give New Mills as their birthplace rather than the parish in which they were born, in which case the figures for Ollersett and whitle are misleading.

Table IX

Birthplace of Inmates 1851-1891

|  | 1851 | 1861 | 1871 | 1881 | 1891 |
|---|---|---|---|---|---|
| Hayfield | 2 | 1 | 5 | 1 | 3 |
| Ollersett | 2 | 0 | 0 | 1 | 0 |
| Thornsett | 0 | 0 | 0 | 4 | 0 |
| Whitle | 1 | 0 | 0 | 0 | 0 |
| New Mills | 1 | 5 | 13 | 13 | 11 |
| Disley | 2 | 7 | 6 | 6 | 2 |
| Mellor | 4 | 4 | 4 | 3 | 4 |
| Derbyshire | 2 | 6 | 6 | 4 | 0 |
| Lancashire | 4 | 1 | 2 | 11 | 3 |
| Yorkshire | 0 | 2 | 0 | 1 | 2 |
| Cheshire | 0 | 2 | 4 | 2 | 5 |
| Midlands | 0 | 0 | 1 | 10 | 2 |
| London | 2 | 1 | 1 | 3 | 0 |
| Ireland | 6 | 1 | 1 | 4 | 4 |
| Scotland | 0 | 0 | 2 | 1 | 1 |
| Total | 27 | 31 | 44 | 64 | 37 |

40

# Workhouse Life

Life in the Victorian workhouse was not meant to be comfortable or easy. Reverend Milman made this clear in the letter he wrote to the Commissioners. Able-bodied men had to pick oakum, while women were expected to do housework, look after the sick and crush stone to produce sand for cleaning. In October 1842 it was minuted that for the first week after entry a man should pick one pound of oakum per day, and after that two pounds per day. In 1845 the entry read "the Workhouse Master can set any fit person to do any task of work, men to pick one pound of oakun in four hours and women to crush one peck of sand in four hours". In 1862 stone breaking and oakum picking were still standard work for the able-bodied in receipt of relief, and it was suggested that a room be set aside for women to sew in. A month later Mr. Smith, Manager of the M.S.L.Railway Canal Company, offered limestone at 2/6 per ton(12p) at the Canal Wharf Wirksmoor (now Newtown) and would allow free use of part of the wharf. The offer was accepted. One hundred tons of limestone was bought and a wooden shed was built to work in. Two dozen round hammers, two large hammers, two picks and two spades were ordered. It was then decided to build a jetty and put in a water spout for the shed and install a stove and pipe. The project proved quite profitable to the Union finances and an outdoor superintendent was appointed at 12/- per week for a trial period of six weeks. Perhaps it was due to this new woek and its profitability that in November 1862 a new slate bath was installed in a bathroom adjoining the wash-house.Clothing marked Hayfield Union Workhouse (or HUW) was provided for the inmates. In 1846, trousers were ordered which were to be made from "printers' blankets or other coarse material" for the vagrants. Clogs and shoes were bought and repaired at Union expense and appear fairly regularly in the "bills paid" entires. There were also entries about boys who had run away in workhouse clothing being charged with stealing it when they were caught.

# Conclusions

This has been a study of one particular workhouse, its building, its Guardians, its Masters and inmates. The rules governing the formation of the Union and the building of the workhouse as well as the manner in which it should be run were all laid down in by the Poor Law Commission and applied nationally. Victorian literature, such as Oliver Twist, painted a very corrupt regime in workhouses, and of course the Scandal of Andover Workhouse, showed that there was corruption and cruelty in workhouses. Oral history has also painted the workhouse as a terrible place, which one kept out of if possible, and as a result the reputations of Guardians and Masters suffered. By looking closely at Hayfield Union Workhouse over the years of its existance, it is possible to shed some light on both the conditions within the workhouse and also on the characters of the Guardians and Masters.

The Guardians were drawn mainly form the businessmen and farmers of the area, as of course in the early years thay were the ones who filled the reqired qualifications. The manufacturers of the area tended to be paternalistic to the workforce and naturally acted in the same way towards those needing relief, indoor or outdoor. The "poor" needed to be told what to do, to be supervised in their work and a watch kept on their morals. Drinking and gambling were frowned upon and anyone found indulging was warned of dire consequences. The Guardians worked hard themselves, but

took their responsibilities seriously as shown by their regular
attendence and long terms in office. To modern eyes they appear
stern and uncaring in expecting able-bodied people to work
picking oakum and stone crushing, but the Victorian work ethic
was very strong, and the use of the terms "deserving" and
"undeserving" poor as guidelines as to who should be helped and
who not, had a strong influence on middle-class Victorians.
However some of the Guardians' decisions regarding the behaviour
of Masters was very strange.They took the word of a Master in
spite of the fact that Magistrates found him guilty and paid his
fine. For seven years they received complaints from inmates and
staff about another Master before they asked for his dismissal.
But there are no signs that the Guardians themselves were corrupt
or cruel, in fact on several occasions they showed great thought
for the welfare of the inmates. Gaurdians and their wives did
their best to improve the reputation of the workhouse especially
after the Local Government Board took over responsibility for
supervising the Poor Law and encouraged a more liberal running of
the workhouses. The only real criticism of the Hayfield Guardians
is that they were procrastinators when it came to building or
altering the buildings to suit new requirements. The idea to
extend the the workhouse by first puchasing more land first came
up in 1884. It took till 1899 for the land to be bought and a
further four years to start the planned extensions!

Of the ten Masters and Matrons of Hayfield Union, the majority
appear to have done their work well.Absence and drunkeness lead

to the resignation of the second Master,while the P.L.B. put
pressure on the third Master to go after he had been convicted of
hitting a man. The seventh Master was considereda hard master,
and caused a Guardian to remark "this is not a prison, but an
asylum for the poor and needy",however he was not asked to resign
in spite of various complaints.The ninth Master would have been
at home in Oliver Twist, (although the work house in that book
was based on a workhouse before the New Poor Law came in) as
would have been his wife the Matron, but it took seven years to
get rid of them. The tenth Master served for twenty eight years
and there is no evidence that he was other than a good master.
Considering that no qualifications were necessary for the
position other than to be "good with accounts" it is not
surprising that some were not really suitable for the job. The
most that can be said for Hayfield Masters is that the majority
ran the workhouse in a reasonable manner within the rules laid
down, and that the inmates didnot suffer from lack of food or
ill-treatment.

Workhouse life is shown as very stark and hard,as it was meant to
deter people from going there if there was any other way they
could feed and cloth themselves and pay for a roof over their
heads.For the old and infirm, it was the last resort when they
ceased to be able to care for themselves and had no relations who
could,or would,look after them. At least they were fed,clothed
and sheltered and were probably better off than if they had not
become inmates. In spite of everything else about the diet,

research shows that the workhouse diet, though boring, offered more food including meat that many working families were able to afford. It was still not a life most wished for or looked forward to, but perhaps it was better than being on the streets starving. Myth, literature and oral history have painted the worst scenario, this study has shown that while the workhouse was not the best place to spend declining years, in Hayfield is was not as bad as that scenario.

# FRONT VIEW OF A WORKHOUSE DESIGNED FOR 300 PAUPERS

Sampson Kempthorne, Architect, Carlton Chambers, 12 Regent St, London.

WORKHOUSE FOR 300 PAUPERS,—GROUND PLAN, No. 1. (F.)

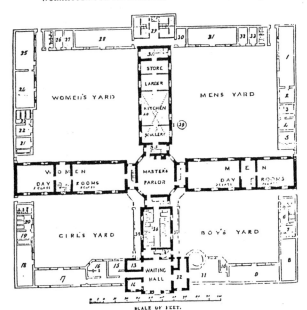

SCALE OF FEET.

| | | |
|---|---|---|
| 1 Work Room. | 15 Store. | 29 Piggery. |
| 2 Store. | 16 Potatoes. | 30 Slaughter House. |
| 3 Receiving Wards, 3 beds. | 17 Coals. | 31 Work Room. |
| 4 Bath. | 18 Work Room. | 32 Refractory Ward. |
| 5 Washing Room. | 19 Washing Room. | 33 Dead House. |
| 6 Receiving Ward, 3 beds. | 20 Receiving Ward, 3 beds. | 34 Women's Stairs to Dining |
| 7 Washing Room. | 21 Washing Room. | Hall. |
| 8 Work Room. | 22 Bath. | 35 Men's Stairs to ditto. |
| 9 Flour and Mill Room. | 23 Receiving Ward, 3 beds. | 36 Boys' and Girls' School |
| 10 Coals. | 24 Laundry. | and Dining Room. |
| 11 Bakehouse. | 25 Wash-house. | 37 Delivery. |
| 12 Bread Room. | 26 Dead House. | 38 Passage. |
| 13 Searching Room. | 27 Refractory Ward. | 39 Well. |
| 14 Porter's Room. | 28 Work Room. | 40 Cellar under ground. |

# THE POOR IN THE HOUSE,

### are required

## TO OBSERVE THE FOLLOWING RULES

I.     That they obey the *Governor* and *Matron* in all their reasonable commands.

II.     That they demean themselves orderley and peaceable, with decency and cleanliness.

III.     That they never drink to excess.

IV.     That they be diligent at their work.

V.     That they work from six o'clock in the morning till six at night, in summer; and from seven o'clock in the morning till such hours in the evening, as the *Directors* shall appoint, in the winter; except *Saturday afternoons*, from four o'clock; and on *Good Friday, Christmas Day*, and the *two days following*, and *Monday* and *Tuesday* in the *Easter* and *Whitsun Weeks*, which are to be regarded as *Holidays*.

VI.     That they do not pretend sickness, or other excuses to avoid their work.

VII.     That they do no wilful damage, but execute their work to the best of their abilities. — Such rewards and gratuities shall be distributed to the industrious and skilful in proportion to the quantity and perfection of their work, as to the *Church-wardens* and *Overseers* shall seem reasonable. *(Man. Act. Sec. 36)*

VIII.     That they regularly attend divine service on *Sundays*, and prayers before breakfast and supper every day.

IX.     That they go to breakfast, to dinner, and to supper, in the *Dining-Hall*, when summoned by ring of bell.

X.     That they be allowed half an hour at breakfast, and an hour at dinner.

XI.     That no strong or spirituous liquors be allowed in the House, except by order of the *Physicians* or *Apothecary*.

XII.     That they do not curse, nor swear, nor lie.

XIII.     That they do not steal, sell their provisions, or sell or pawn their cloathing, nor be guilty of any other breach of trust.

XIV.     That they never go out during working-hours, nor at any other time, without leave.

XV.     That when permitted to go out, they do not stay longer than the hour appointed.

WHOEVER shall offend against the above Rules, will be punished either by confinement in the stocks, or in the dungeon, or elsewhere, or by distinction of dress, by abatement of diet, loss of gratuity, by such corporal or other punishment as may be determined and adjudged by the *Weekly Board of Overseers*, according to the powers vested in them by the Act of Parliament.

These Rules shall be read to the Poor in the House by the *Governor* on the first *Monday* in every month.

Manchester

Notes

1. Trevor May The Victorian Workhouse Shire Publications Ltd. p 6

2. M.A.Crowther The Workhouse System Methuen Paperback 1983 p 269

3. Ian Anstruther The Scandal of Andover Workhouse Alan Sutton
   Publishing Ltd. 1984

4. M.A.Crowther p 45

5. John Cole Down Poor House Lane pub. Geo. Kelsall p 13

6. M.A.Crowther p 47

7. D441/C/W Guardian Minute Books Derbyshire Records Office
   1837-1930 MH12 204 Poor Law Correspondence 1835-1900 Public
   Records Office

8. Poor Law Correspondence February 1838

9. M.E.Rose The English Poor Law 1780-1930 Paperback Edition p1

10. M.A.Crowther introduction

11. Poor Law Ammendment Act 1834

12. Poor Law Correspondence 12 october 1835

13. Minute Books and Poor Law Correspondence

14. "       "       "    "    "         "

15. Poor Law Correspondence 11 January 1838

16. "    "       "         27 December 1837

17. "    "       "         10 November 1838

18. J.L.Perry Lancaster University Poor Law and Kendal Union p 4

19. Ian Ansruther p 24

20. M.Caplan In the Shadow of the Workhouse Univerity of
    Nottingham Paper no 3 p 53

21. Ian Anstruther

22. M.Caplan

23.Glossopdale Chronicle January 1902

24.Guardian Minutes and Poor Law Correspondence June 1897

25.Glossopdale Chronicle January/February 1902

26.Article 189 of General Consolidation Order Poor Law
Correspondence

27.Ashton Reporter 28 August 1897

28.M.A.Crowther p 41

All information in the chapter on inmates is from the Minute
Books, Poor Law Correspondence and the Enumerator's books of the
Censuses 1851-1891 inclusive

Plans 131250/98, 15046/96 and 1855 drawing are by courtesy of the
Public Records Office

Dietary Tables October 1856, Abstract showing numbers of
paupersand expenditure courtesy of the Public Records Office

Rules for Paupers in the Workhouse and Plan of workhouse for 300
paupers by courtesy of the Derbyshire Records Office